THE ALTAR MINISTRY

A Call To The Sacred Place

By

Nina Brown

TABLE OF CONTENTS

DEDICATION

Thank You, Lord, for Your infinite love, guidance, grace, and mercy.

You are the source of every word I write and every step I take.

Thank You for calling me to Your altar,

For entrusting me with the sacred work of serving You,

And for allowing me to be a vessel of Your power and glory.

All honor, praise, and glory belong to You

Chapter 1

THE SACRED ALTAR

T his book is written with the altar worker in mind, to provide a deeper understanding of the sacred role they play in the Kingdom of God. For those who stand at the altar, their service is not just a physical act but a spiritual responsibility that impacts eternity. The altar is a place where God's presence is encountered, where divine transactions are made between God and man, and where transformation happens.

As we explore the significance of altar ministry, this book will guide you in recognizing the weight and power of your service. It will help you understand how your role as an altar worker aligns with God's greater purposes, empowering you to serve with greater reverence, respect and honor in the presence of God at the altar.

Through these pages, you will discover how your commitment to the altar has eternal implications, as it is a place where heaven touches earth, and lives are forever changed.

Let's begin

What is an Altar?

The Sacred Altar: A Place of Divine Encounter

Make an altar of earth for me and sacrifice on it your burnt offerings and fellowship offerings, your sheep and goats and your cattle. Wherever I cause my name to be honored, I will come to you and bless you. (Exodus 20:24)

The altar is a sacred meeting place between God and man—a place of sacrifice, surrender, and worship. It is where offerings are presented to God, symbolizing reverence, devotion, and obedience. More than a physical structure, the altar represents a divine connection where God's presence manifests, blessings flow, and lives are transformed.

In Genesis 12:7, we see the profound significance of the altar:

The LORD appeared to Abram and said, 'To your offspring I will give this land.' So he built an altar there to the LORD, who had appeared to him.

Abram's altar marked a sacred encounter, a site where heaven met earth, and God's promise was declared. It was a place dedicated to the Lord, marked for supernatural visitation. The altar is where divine transactions are made—where spiritual purposes are executed, prayers are answered, and destinies are shaped.

The altar is not just a physical location; it is a place of honor, consecration, and holy exchange. It is where:

Heaven meets earth to execute spiritual purposes.

God manifests Himself to deliver, heal, and restore His people.

Humanity surrenders and receives guidance, strength, and renewal.

For those called to altar ministry, understanding the significance of this sacred place is vital. The altar is where God's glory meets human need, where worshipers encounter Him in transformative ways. It is a space of supernatural visitation, where the Lord draws near to bless and empower His people.

Serving at the altar is not a task to be taken lightly. It requires reverence, preparation, and a clear sense of purpose to carry out the divine assignments entrusted to you.

The altar is holy ground—a space where divinity connects with humanity, and God's purposes are revealed and fulfilled. Embrace its sacredness, and you will witness lives changed, prayers answered, and heaven's power released in extraordinary ways.

Chapter 2

THE WORK OF THE HOLY SPIRIT AND YOUR ROLE AS AN ALTAR WORKER

For we are co-workers in God's service (1Corinthian 3:9)

The Holy Spirit is our greatest helper in ministry. Holy Spirit is the primary agent at work at the altar. Every movement, every prayer, and every manifestation flows from Him. Understanding how to assist Him is important for the flow of the altar ministry.

Not by might nor by power but by my Spirit says the LORD Almighty (Zechariah 4:6)

As altar workers, we must rely on His guidance in all we do. Understanding that we partner with God actively participating along side the Holy Spirit, to build His church.

As an Altar worker you are called to steward the sacred space, your actions facilitate others encounters with God, whether catching, praying or holding the oil, you should have a posture of humility and reverence with a readiness to serve.

Understanding your role at the altar is essential for effective service. It is important to recognize that within the altar ministry, there are distinct roles, each with its own function, responsibility, and level of authority. The altar operates as a place of reverence and divine interaction, where all workers must be aware of their specific duties and the spiritual ranks they hold.

Humility and reverence in the presence of God are key to honoring the structure of the altar. By embracing your specific role, you not only serve God faithfully, but you also contribute to the spiritual order and harmony that God desires for His people.

I will build my church and the gates of hades shall not prevail against it. (Mathew 16:18)

Through the work of altar workers the church is built and the Kingdom advances

Chapter 3

A GATEWAY TO DIVINE ENCOUNTERS

———

Heaven is actively moving at this heavenly realm called the altar. It is where the divine intersects with the earthly, where God's presence is tangibly felt, and where His actions manifest in powerful ways. Throughout Scripture, the altar serves as a place where God's will is executed, His power is released, and His promises are fulfilled.

The altar is a meeting point between natural and supernatural. This sacred place is where the natural realm intersects with the supernatural. Just as Jacob had a vision of heaven opened above him at Bethel, the altar serves as a gateway for divine revelation and spiritual encounters.

Jacob saw a ladder connecting earth and heaven, with angels ascending and descending, symbolizing God's active involvement in the affairs of humanity (Genesis 28:12-17).

In awe of the experience, Jacob declared, Surely the LORD is in this place, and I was not aware of it. How awesome is this place! This is none other than the house of God; this is the gate of heaven(Genesis 28:16-17).

For altar workers, this truth holds significant meaning. The altar is more than a place of sacrifice—it is a portal for divine transactions where:

- Heaven's resources are released to empower lives.
- Spiritual purposes are established, and prayers are answered.
- Deliverance, healing, and breakthroughs take place.

By serving at the altar, you become a steward of this sacred connection. It is a privilege and responsibility to facilitate moments where others can encounter God's presence in transformative ways. Understanding this role elevates the importance of preparation, humility, and obedience as you assist in creating an atmosphere for divine visitation.

The altar remains a place of awe and reverence, where God reveals His glory and heaven touches earth. As an altar worker, your dedication to preserving its sanctity is vital to its purpose being fulfilled.

Divine Encounters at the Altar

The altar is a place where heaven responds to the prayers and sacrifices of God's people. Throughout the Bible, we see how altars became the meeting point for divine encounters:

Abraham experienced God's promise at the altar.

Then the Lord appeared to Abram and said, 'To your descendants, I will give this land.' And there he built an altar to the Lord, who had appeared to him. (Genesis 12:7)

At the altar, Abraham not only communed with God but also received a covenantal promise that would impact generations.

Cornelius encountered the supernatural through his prayers and offerings.

About the ninth hour of the day, he clearly saw in a vision an angel of God who had come to him and said, 'Cornelius! ... Your prayers and gifts to the poor have ascended as a memorial offering before God. (Acts 10:3-6)

Cornelius' devotion at the altar triggered an angelic visitation and the outpouring of the Holy Spirit on his household, marking a pivotal moment in the spread of the Gospel.

The altar remains a sacred space where prayers ascend, and heaven moves in response. It is a place of divine connection, where God's presence is revealed, promises are fulfilled, and the power of the Holy Spirit is poured out. Whether through Abraham's covenant or Cornelius' breakthrough, the altar demonstrates the life-changing impact of encounters with God.

Spiritual Warfare at the Altar: Elijah's Battle on Mount Carmel

In 1 Kings 18 :20-40 Elijah engages in a powerful battle of spiritual warfare at the altar. The altar became the battlefield between the true God of Israel and the false god Baal. Elijah rebuilds the altar of the Lord, which had been

broken down, and prepares a sacrifice, while challenging the prophets of Baal to do the same.

As an altar worker, you are not merely serving in a physical location but, you are part of the heavenly host, engaging in spiritual warfare alongside the angels of God.

The altar is a sacred battlefield where divine intervention takes place, and lives are transformed. When you stand at the altar, you are operating from a heavenly dimension, where God's power is actively moving to break chains, destroy strongholds, and usher in His will.

This is why order and preparedness are crucial. Spiritual warfare requires focus, humility, and sensitivity to the Holy Spirit. The anointing flows through vessels who are spiritually prepared, aligned with God, and ready to assist Him in the work of deliverance, healing, and salvation.

At the altar, your role is more than just physical service it is a spiritual partnership with heaven. Angels are present, ministering to those in need and warring against the forces of darkness. Your obedience and reverence ensure that you are in sync with this divine operation, creating an atmosphere where heaven can move freely.

Being an altar worker is not just a duty; it is a high calling to co-labor with God and His heavenly armies in advancing His kingdom and bringing His people into victory.

The power of order at the altar

Being spiritually ordered as an altar worker includes learning to respect and honor your co-laborers. The altar is a place of divine partnership, not only with heaven but also with those who serve alongside you. Unity among altar workers creates an environment where the Holy Spirit can move freely, and the power of God is unhindered.

Respecting each other's roles and leadership is critical. Each person has a unique assignment, whether it is catching, holding the oil, praying, or assisting in other ways. These roles are not about status but about fulfilling God's purpose with excellence. When everyone honors their part and values the contributions of others, the altar functions in divine harmony, reflecting the heavenly order.

Disrespect, competition, or a lack of submission to leadership disrupts the flow. The altar ministry requires humility and a servant's heart, where the focus remains on God's work, recognizing the authority of leadership and maintaining a spirit of peace will ensure that the altar remains a place of reverence, power, and victory.

By respecting one another and staying in alignment, you fulfill your calling as a co-laborer in Christ, creating a sacred space where heaven's agenda is accomplished.

Chapter 4

THE ACTIVITY OF ANGELS AT THE ALTAR

Then an angel of the Lord appeared to him, standing at the right side of the altar of incense. When Zechariah saw him, he was startled and was gripped with fear. But the angel said to him: 'Do not be afraid, Zechariah; your prayer has been heard. Your wife Elizabeth will bear you a son, and you are to call him John. (Luke 1:11-13)

At the altar, angels are actively at work, bringing heaven's power to earth in amazing ways.

These divine messengers aren't just watching they're involved in every moment, assisting with prayers, carrying out God's will, and bringing breakthrough.

When we stand at the altar, we're not just doing spiritual business on our own; angels are there, helping to release God's power, healing, and deliverance. Their presence makes our prayers stronger, our worship deeper, and our intercession more effective. Knowing that angels are working alongside us should fill us with awe and expectation, knowing that heaven is backing our every move as we serve at the altar. Their activity reminds us that the altar is not just a place of human effort, but a powerful, supernatural encounter where angels are busy carrying out God's plans.

This passage shows Gabriel, an angel, appearing to Zechariah at the altar of incense while he was fulfilling his priestly duty. Gabriel's presence demonstrates the divine involvement of angels in altar ministry, affirming that they assist in carrying out God's purposes, delivering messages, and responding to the prayers offered at the altar.

Another angel, who had a golden censer, came and stood at the altar. He was given much incense to offer, with the prayers of all God's people, on the golden altar in front of the throne. (Revelation 8:3)

This verse reveals the significant role angels play at the altar, as they assist in presenting the prayers of believers before God. It shows the sacredness of altar ministry and highlights how angels work alongside those serving in spiritual roles, elevating the prayers and intercession of God's people.

Chapter 5

HOLINESS AT THE ALTAR: NO FLESH ALLOWED

Aaron's sons Nadab and Abihu took their censers, put fire in them and added incense; and they offered unauthorized fire before the Lord, contrary to His command. So fire came out from the presence of the Lord and consumed them, and they died before the Lord. Moses then said to Aaron, 'This is what the Lord spoke of when he said: Among those who approach me I will be proved holy; in the sight of all the people I will be honored.' Aaron remained silent (Leviticus 10:1-2)

Aaron's sons remind us that altar ministry is not about your personal agenda; it is about aligning with God's will and maintaining the sanctity of the altar.

When we come to the altar, we must present ourselves holy before God. The flesh must be denied for the Spirit of God to move freely.

Aaron's sons, Nadab and Abihu, were priests called to serve at the altar with sacred responsibilities, including offering incense as part of their duties. However, they made a grave error by offering unauthorized or "strange fire"—a fire not commanded by God. In doing so, they stepped into the role of their father, Aaron, the high priest, who alone was authorized by God to maintain the fire on the altar. Their role was to support Aaron, not to assume his responsibilities. Because they acted without God's authorization, judgment came upon them immediately.

Serving at the altar requires strict adherence to God's instructions and holiness. Nadab and Abihu approached the altar casually and with disobedience, leading to their judgment.

Reverence and Obedience: This account demonstrates that those serving at the altar must treat it with utmost respect, following God's commands faithfully respecting the order and ranks so there is no confusion no disruption at the sacred place.

Application for Altar Workers Today

This story serves as a warning and a guide for modern altar workers. The altar is a sacred place where God's presence is manifest, and those who serve must be spiritually prepared, consecrated, and obedient to God's instructions. Casual and unprepared service can disrupt the flow of the Holy Spirit and dishonor God. Don't ever feel over familiar with the altar it is a place of Holiness and the Holy Spirit is there ministering and working in the lives of people.

Chapter 6

PREPARING YOUR HEART FOR THE ALTAR MINISTRY

Therefore, if anyone cleanses himself from what is dishonorable he will be a vessel for honorable use, set apart as holy, useful to the master of the house, ready for every good work (2 Timothy 2:21)

This implies those Serving in ministry including altar work must approach their assignment with intentionality and reverence before the Lord. To ensure you are spiritually prepared.

The altar worker needs to understand that this is not just a task but a spiritual service that requires a prepared heart.

Before preparing the altar for others, we must first prepare our hearts by making it the first altar we build. Personal preparation is key to effectively serving in altar ministry; you need sensitivity to the Holy Spirit and to the people He is ministering to. In order to develop this sensitivity you need to have your own personal prayer life and a prayer life connecting with the local assembly you serve. This is spiritual preparation so that you are effective and honorable in service to God

Preparing Yourself as an Altar Worker: A Sacred Responsibility

As an altar worker, the call to serve is not merely a role—it is a divine assignment that demands spiritual preparation. Before stepping into this sacred space, you must consecrate yourself, aligning your heart, mind, and spirit with God. The altar is where heaven touches earth, where battles are fought, and where lives are transformed. To serve effectively, you must approach with reverence, humility, and readiness.

1. Spiritual Cleansing

Psalm 24:3-4 reminds us: Who may ascend the hill of the Lord? Who may stand in His holy place? The one who has clean hands and a pure heart.

Before approaching the altar, ensure your heart is free from offenses, unforgiveness, or unrepented sin. Spend time in prayer, asking the Holy Spirit to search you and cleanse you of anything that might hinder His work through you.

2. Fasting and Prayer

Spiritual warfare at the altar requires power, and power comes through prayer and fasting. Jesus said in Matthew 17:21, This kind does not go out except by prayer and fasting." Taking time to fast and pray before serving prepares you to partner with the Holy Spirit and align with His authority.

3. Spiritual Armor

Put on the whole armor of God, as described in Ephesians 6:10-18. Serving at the altar means stepping into spiritual warfare. Protect yourself by standing in truth, righteousness, faith, and the Word of God, so you can resist any attacks from the enemy.

4. Sensitivity to the Holy Spirit

The altar is a place of divine encounter. To serve effectively, you must be in tune with the Holy Spirit's leading. Be prayerful and watchful, asking for discernment so that your actions and prayers align with His purpose for each person who comes to the altar.

5. Respect for the Sacredness of the Altar

Approach the altar with a deep understanding of its significance. It is not a place for personal agendas, casual attitudes, or disunity. Respect the leadership, the roles of your co-laborers, and most importantly, the presence of God.

Preparation is the foundation of effective altar ministry. When you prepare yourself spiritually, you create a vessel through which God's power can flow unhindered. The altar worker must understand that their readiness impacts the lives of those seeking God at the altar. It is a high calling, and preparation ensures you honor it with the reverence it deserves.

Know that your role weather catching, holding the oil, or praying are all vital roles in supporting the flow of the Holy Spirit; therefore, spend time in prayer before serving. the altar.

Understand the altar ministry isn't just a task but a spiritual service that requires a prepared heart

Your role as an altar worker shows unity and support for the church's spiritual leadership.

As you are complementing your Pastors who are ministering for the people they serve in the congregation The altar workers are reflection of the church they serve and show the kind of leadership they serve under.

Chapter 7

REWARDS FOR SERVING GOD AT THE ALTAR

For God is not unjust; He will not forget your work and the love you have shown Him as you have helped His people and continue to help them. (Hebrews 6:1)

Serving God at the altar is a sacred duty that comes with both spiritual and eternal rewards. Those who dedicate themselves to this ministry experience the blessing of partnering with the Holy Spirit to bring about life-changing encounters for others. Below are the key rewards of faithfully serving God at the altar:

The Presence of God

Serving at the altar allows you to experience God's presence in a deeper and more profound way The altar is the place where the presence of God is active, where the kingdom of God operates to destroy the works of darkness and bring freedom and deliverance to the people seeking God's help.

As an altar worker in any capacity, you are invited to be a conduit of this power and a recipient of the glory of God.

When you understand the significance of His presence at the altar as a direct connection between God and man, you will approach the altar with a new respect. Having this reverence not only honors God but also positions you to experience His glory. Because the presence of God dwells at the altar, serving there is both a privilege and an honor, allowing you as a steward to cater to the presence of the Almighty.

You make known to me the path of life; you will fill me with joy in your presence, with eternal pleasures at your right hand. (Psalm 16:11)

Those who serve at the altar encounter the fullness of joy that comes from dwelling in His presence.

Growth in Spiritual Authority

Faithful service at the altar often results in an increase in spiritual authority. When you align with God's will, He entrusts you with more responsibilities and power to minister effectively.

Luke 16:10: "Whoever can be trusted with very little can also be trusted with much.

As you remain faithful in small acts of service, God expands your influence and equips you for greater assignments in His kingdom.

Eternal Rewards For Altar Workers

Altar ministry has eternal significance. Every prayer you pray, every person you help under the anointing, and every act of service is recorded in heaven.

But store up for yourselves treasures in heaven, where moths and vermin do not destroy, and where thieves do not break in and steal. (Matthew 6:20)

Your work at the altar has a ripple effect, influencing lives for eternity and contributing to the expansion of God's kingdom.

The Blessing of Witnessing Transformation

One of the most rewarding aspects of altar ministry is seeing lives transformed by the power of God. You witness firsthand the deliverance, healing, and breakthroughs that happen when people surrender their burdens at the altar.

Therefore, if anyone is in Christ, the new creation has come: The old has gone, the new is here! (2 Corinthians 5:17)

Every testimony of transformation affirms the importance of your role in assisting the Holy Spirit.

Personal Renewal and Strength

As you pour out to others in ministry, God pours into you. Serving at the altar is a humbling experience that draws you closer to God and renews your own spiritual strength.

But those who hope in the Lord will renew their strength. They will soar on wings like eagles; they will run and not grow weary, they will walk and not be faint. (Isaiah 40:31)

Your service does not deplete you; instead, it allows God to fill you anew.

Favor and Recognition from God

God acknowledges and rewards the sacrifices made by those who serve Him faithfully. While people may not always see your labor, God sees and honors your faithfulness.

Whatever you do, work at it with all your heart, as working for the Lord, not for human masters, since you know that you will receive an inheritance from the Lord as a reward.
(Colossians 3:23-24)

God's favor on your life is a direct result of your unwavering commitment to His work.

Serving God at the altar requires humility, preparation, and obedience. It may be demanding at times, but the rewards far outweigh the sacrifices. Each time you serve, remember that you are partnering with God in transforming lives and building His kingdom. Your labor is never in vain, and the blessings, both here and in eternity, are immeasurable.

Stay steadfast in your calling, knowing that your work at the altar is precious in God's sight and carries eternal significance.

Serving at the altar is not only a privilege, but it also comes with heavenly rewards. The impact of our work at the altar is eternal.

The rewards for serving God at the altar extend far beyond what we can imagine. They enrich your life here on earth and lay the foundation for an eternal inheritance in heaven. Faithful service not only glorifies God but also brings fulfillment, blessings, and spiritual empowerment to your life.

Chapter 8

LESSONS FROM ZECHARIAH A PRIEST AT THE ALTAR

Once when Zechariah's division was on duty and he was serving as priest before God, he was chosen by lot, according to the custom of the priesthood, to go into the temple of the Lord and burn incense. And when the time for the burning of incense came, all the assembled worshipers were praying outside. Then an angel of the Lord appeared to him, standing at the right side of the altar of incense. When Zechariah saw him, he was startled and was gripped with fear. But the angel said to him. Do not be afraid, Zechariah; your prayer has been heard. Your wife Elizabeth will bear you a son, and you are to call him John.(Luke 1:8-13)

Zechariah's service in the temple reveals significant lessons for those who serve at the altar. As a priest, Zechariah was diligent and faithful in his ministry. Though he waited long for the promise had not been fulfilled, he remained committed to his duties at the altar. This demonstrates that altar workers should serve honorably and faithfully in their roles, even when personal desires and prayers seem unanswered.

Zechariah's faithfulness as an altar worker teaches us the power of consistency. He didn't allow the waiting a long time or his unfulfilled prayers to hinder his service. Altar workers should learn from his example, understanding that every moment of service, no matter how ordinary it seems, is significant in God's plan.

Zechariah's turn to minister at the altar shows the privilege and responsibility of being in the presence of God. When we come to the altar, we do so not only to serve but to stand in a sacred place where God works, Just as Zechariah's encounter with the angel occurred in his role as a priest at the altar, altar workers can be assured that their service in the sacred altar is never in vain. God meets us at the altar, and it is through our faithful service that we align with His divine purpose.

The story of Zechariah shows us that altar workers are crucial in the working of God's will. Their obedience and dedication to the sacred task of the altar ministry, even when unseen or unrecognized, position them to be part of something much greater than themselves. The altar is a place of consecration and alignment with God's purposes, and those who serve there are part of His divine plan unfolding.

Through Zechariah's example, altar workers are reminded that their service is valuable, their faithfulness matters, and God will honor those who remain diligent in their sacred duties at the altar.

Chapter 9

THE LEGACY OF THE ALTAR WORKER

————————

They shall be on Aaron and his sons when they go into the
tent of meeting, or when they come near the altar to minister
in to The holy place, that they do not incur guilt and die. This
is a statute forever for him and for his offspring after him,
(Exodus 28:43)

Aarons lineage was responsible for offering sacrifices, maintaining the sacredness of the altar.

In leaving a legacy, altar workers must also mentor others. Pouring into the next generation ensures that the work of the altar continues with integrity, power, and reverence. Teach others to honor the sacredness of the altar and to serve with humility and holiness, just as Aaron passed down the responsibilities of the priesthood to his sons.

Every act of service at the altar carries profound importance, contributing to the Kingdom of God and leaving a legacy that outlasts us. From the intercessor standing in the gap for others, to the one catching those under the power of the anointing, to those holding the anointing oil, to those used to exhortation every role is sacred and vital.

The legacy we create through our work at the altar is both spiritual and eternal, and it sets the foundation for greater works to come for you and your children all for generations to come.

Roles of an Altar Worker

The Intercessor: Intercessors at the altar are spiritual warriors, partnering with the Holy Spirit to bring about breakthrough in the lives of others. Their prayers create an atmosphere of faith, driving back darkness and ushering in God's presence. These unseen battles bear fruit not only in the moment but in the eternal destinies of those for whom they pray.

The Catcher: Those who catch individuals under the power of the anointing perform a ministry of care and reverence. They ensure that people touched by the Spirit are handled with dignity and safety, maintaining order as God's power is displayed. This seemingly simple task is an act of humility and servant leadership.

The Holder of the Oil: The oil represents the presence and power of the Holy Spirit, and those entrusted to hold it demonstrate stewardship of what is sacred. This role reflects deep reverence for God's anointing and attention to detail in serving His people.

The Prayer Leader: Leading prayers at the altar is an act of guidance, drawing people into alignment with God's will. It requires a heart attuned to the Holy Spirit and sensitivity to the needs of those present, ensuring the altar remains a place of healing, deliverance, and restoration.

Teaching, preaching, exhortation : Some altar workers are called to provide service of exhortation. preaching teaching prophesying. Their role is to uplift those who are weary or broken, speaking life and hope into their situations. These ministries are serviced at the Sacred Altar of the Most High God, has lasting impact as it breathes fresh faith into individuals.

Each of these roles, though distinct, contributes to the sacred work of the altar. Just as Abraham's obedience to God established a covenant that impacted generations, so too does the work of altar workers create ripples of transformation. When we minister under the anointing of the Holy Spirit, we are planting seeds of healing, restoration, and purpose that will grow long after our service ends.

The legacy also extends beyond what is visible. Many altar workers in Scripture, like Zechariah, faithfully fulfilled their duties, not fully understanding the fullness of God's plans. Faithfulness in these tasks reflects humility and a commitment to the sacredness of altar ministry.

Your legacy is built on your consistent acts of faithfulness. The work you do at the altar is precious to God. Serve with an eternal perspective, knowing that your efforts contribute to the expansion of His Kingdom and the fulfillment of His promises.

Chapter 10

THE BLOODLINE BLESSING OF THE ALTAR WORKER

Now take Aaron your brother, and his sons with him, from among the children of Israel, that he may minister to Me as priest, Aaron and Aaron's sons: Nadab, Abihu, Eleazar, and Ithamar. (Exodus 28:1)

This verse highlights God's selection of Aaron and his sons for the sacred duty of priesthood, serving at the altar and ministering before Him. As altar workers, the ministry of serving at the altar became a part of the bloodline inheritance, a gift that became a legacy of Aaron's descendants. This divine calling was not just a role for Aaron but a generational anointing that would pass through his lineage.

In our obedience to God, as we serve at the altar, it opens doors to a bloodline blessing that extends to our children and beyond. The anointing we carry today can impact not only our own lives but also the generations to come. Just as God honored the faithfulness of Aaron and his sons, He honors the obedience of those who serve in His house, promising blessings that extend through family lines.

The Blood of Jesus and the Altar Worker

The anointing of Aaron and his sons is a powerful illustration of consecration. They were washed, clothed in priestly garments, and anointed with sacred oil. The blood of the sacrificial ram was applied to Aaron's right ear, thumb, and toe, signifying the consecration of hearing, service, and walking before the Lord. This act demonstrated the seriousness of their role in the service of the altar, as they were being set apart to minister in God's presence.

As altar workers today, we are reminded of the power of the blood of Jesus Christ, which fulfills the ultimate sacrifice. While the blood of the ram consecrated Aaron and his sons for service, the blood of Jesus Christ cleanses and consecrates us, empowering us to serve in the heavenly priesthood. Through His blood, we have been washed clean, anointed for service, and sanctified to carry out the work at the altar with purity and reverence. The blood of Jesus is the ultimate blessing, covering us, consecrating our ears to hear His voice, our hands to serve, and our feet to walk in His will, just as it did for Aaron and his sons.

The blood of Jesus not only purifies us but also aligns us with the divine authority required to fulfill our roles at the altar. As we serve, we tap into the eternal power of Christ's sacrifice, enabling us to stand firm in our calling. This sacred bloodline blessing empowers us to walk in authority, ensuring that every act of service, no matter how small, carries weight in the spirit. Through this sacred lineage, we are connected to a heavenly heritage, walking in the footsteps of those who have faithfully ministered before us and carrying forward the blessings God has promised to His obedient servants.

In the same way that the lineage of Aaron was marked by God's favor and blessing, we too have a spiritual inheritance through our service at the altar. Our children and grandchildren will be impacted by our dedication, and the favor of God will rest upon them as they witness our faithful service and live in the blessings of the covenant.

Just as Aaron's bloodline carried the blessing of the priesthood, so too do we, as altar workers, carry the blessing of God's divine presence and calling. Through our service, we are actively participating in the unfolding of God's redemptive plan and establishing a legacy of faithfulness, obedience, and blessing that will be passed on to future generations.

The Power of Consecration Through the Blood of Jesus

The blood of Jesus is powerful and transformative. It is the blood that cleanses, consecrates, and empowers us as altar workers. It is the blood that sets us apart for the sacred work of the altar, enabling us to serve in purity, holiness, and with the anointing of the Holy Spirit. Without the blood, we would be unworthy to stand before God and fulfill the high calling of altar ministry.

Altar Workers Are Set apart for a higher purpose

The Lord gave a clear instruction to Aaron and his sons: You and your sons are not to drink wine or other fermented drink whenever you go into the tent of meeting, or you will die. This is a lasting ordinance for the generations to come, so that you can distinguish between the holy and the common, between the unclean and the clean(Leviticus 10:8-11).

This commandment highlights the sacred nature of the altar and the necessity for those who serve in it to be consecrated, set apart, and spiritually prepared.

As altar workers, our calling goes beyond physical service; we are partaking in a divine lineage sealed by the blood of Christ. This sacred calling is not only about performing duties but engaging in the spiritual purpose that God has laid before us. Just as Zechariah's faithful service at the altar led to the miraculous birth of John the Baptist, our service, no matter how unseen, releases divine purposes that transform lives and build God's kingdom.

The role of an altar worker demands more than physical presence—it requires spiritual discernment. Workers must have the ability to distinguish between what is holy and what is not, aligning themselves with the Holy Spirit. This discernment is essential for working in harmony with the angels who are present to assist in God's purposes. The altar becomes a sacred space where heaven meets earth, and the Holy Spirit moves freely to minister to those in need.

The blood of Jesus grants us the privilege to serve at the altar. Just as Aaron's sons were chosen to carry the blessings of God, we are appointed with a spiritual heritage to carry His presence and power. The role of an altar worker is a high calling, one that requires dedication, humility, and consecration. It is a responsibility to be spiritually distinct and to serve with a heart of reverence, ensuring that the altar remains a place where God's will is accomplished.

When an altar worker serves with purity, discernment, and obedience, they create a sacred space where the Holy Spirit can move unhindered, where angels assist in the divine work, and where God's kingdom advances. This is a ministry not of mere duty, but of partnership with heaven. Altar workers carry the weight of eternal significance, and their service will be rewarded in the presence of the Lord.

Chapter 11

THE ALTAR MINISTRY A CATALYST FOR SPIRTUAL GROWTH

Seven days you shall make atonement for the altar and consecrate it, and the altar shall be most holy. Whatever touches the altar shall become Holy (Exodus 29)

S erving at the altar brings individuals into a place of preparation for spiritual growth sometimes other ministry responsibilities and new levels of service. The Sacred altar is a place where the Holy Spirit moves powerfully, it also prepares us for greater responsibilities and roles within the body of Christ.

Servicing the altar carries eternal significance. Altar work is not in vain; it is part of God's divine plan, and it impacts the lives of those they serve. By serving at the altar, they are part of something much larger than themselves an eternal work that will continue to bear fruit long after they have finished their service.altar ministry is not only a place of consecration but also a platform for the release of greater anointing as individuals align themselves with God's divine purpose

Applause from Heaven !

Altar workers may never fully understand the eternal impact of their service, but every prayer, every act of obedience, every step taken in reverence for God's presence has an eternal reward. Their legacy is one of faithfulness, devotion, and a commitment to advancing God's Kingdom

As an altar worker, no matter your role, you are appointed to serve in a sacred place, to serve alongside angels, to partner and co labor with the Holy Spirit. You are called to be a light in darkness, standing as a vessel of divine authority and spiritual power. Through your service, you participate in the supernatural work of God, ushering in His presence and facilitating His will on earth. Whether you are holding the oil, praying, or serving in any other capacity, you are an integral part of the spiritual operations that take place in this holy space.

Your role at the altar is a privilege and a calling that carries weight and significance. Your assignment at the altar serves as the catalyst for your supernatural elevation, as God observes and evaluates the quality of your service to take you to the next level of service for the expansion of His kingdom.

As you serve, know that you are part of eternal work that will bear fruit in your account. Your faithfulness is the driving force for supernatural elevation.

Chapter 12

WELL DONE, GOOD AND FAITHFUL SERVANT

———◦◦◦———

In Matthew 25:21, the master commended the servant saying, "Well done, good and faithful servant; you have been faithful with a few things; I will put you in charge of many things. Come and share your master's happiness." This passage encapsulates the heart of service at the altar— faithful service that pleases God.

As altar workers, you are not just performing a duty; you are participating in a divine calling. Every act of service, no matter how small or unseen, is significant in God's eyes. The prayers you offer, the hands you lay upon others, the way you uphold the atmosphere of reverence—all are part of the sacred work that God honors.

Your faithfulness to God's call at the altar is not measured by the visibility of your actions but by your obedience to His voice and your reverence for the sacredness of the work. Even when no one sees your efforts or the struggles you face in the background, God sees. He recognizes the heart of a servant, willing to labor in His house with humility and dedication.

The beauty of being an altar worker is that your service doesn't go unnoticed. While the applause of the world may be fleeting, there is an eternal applause from Heaven for every faithful servant. It is the applause that comes from the Father's heart, the kind that echoes through the heavens, declaring "Well done, good and faithful servant." It is the recognition that matters most—the applause that signifies your eternal place in God's Kingdom.

When we serve in the altar ministry, we are working for an eternal reward. This reward may not always be visible in the present, but the Bible assures us that God is faithful to reward those who serve Him with diligence and integrity. And while the applause of man is often driven by pride and recognition, the applause from Heaven is pure—it's the honor of being noticed by the Creator of the universe, whose love and favor transcend earthly accolades.

Every moment you serve at the altar is a step toward fulfilling God's divine purpose. The altar is where destinies are shaped, lives are changed, and God's will is done. As you remain faithful in the small things, you position yourself for greater things in God's Kingdom.

In the end, it's not the titles or the recognition from others that matter; it's the applause from Heaven that echoes through eternity. The glory of His presence, the reward of His well-pleased declaration, and the joy of knowing you've been part of His redemptive work are the ultimate rewards. The altar worker who remains faithful will hear the words that every servant longs for: "Well done, good and faithful servant."

May you, as an altar worker, continue to serve with humility, reverence, and faithfulness, knowing that every action you take, no matter how small, is seen by Heaven. And in the end, it is that eternal applause—the applause from Heaven—that will truly matter.

Conclusion

Your service at the altar is more than a duty—it is a sacred trust and a divine calling. Every prayer lifted, every act of obedience, and every moment you spend in God's presence is a seed sown into eternity. Though your work may seem small or unseen, it holds eternal significance in advancing God's kingdom and touching lives.

At the altar, you are a vessel through which heaven meets earth, a channel for God's power to transform, refine, and empower His people. Your faithfulness not only impacts those you serve but also builds a spiritual legacy that echoes into eternity. The altar is a place where divine purposes are activated and lives are touched by the presence of God. Every prayer, every act of obedience, every moment spent in reverence adds to the greater work that God is doing in the earth.

Never underestimate the weight of your assignment. As you stand in humility, reverence, and dedication, you co-labor with Christ in His redemptive work. The altar is not merely a place of physical service; it is a holy ground where the supernatural and the natural converge. It is where your acts of faith become part of God's eternal plan, and where His presence is made tangible to those around you. Each moment of service at the altar is a testimony of God's faithfulness and power in your life, and a reflection of your commitment to His will.

One day, in the presence of the King, you will hear the words that every servant of God longs to hear: "Well done, good and faithful servant. Enter into the joy of your Lord!" These words will be a celebration of your obedience, your devotion, and your unwavering service in the Kingdom. The reward for your labor may not always be visible here on earth, but the eternal fruit of your service will be evident in the lives that have been touched and transformed by your obedience.

Your service matters, your obedience matters, and your calling matters. Keep serving with excellence, knowing that what you do at the altar is for His glory and will be rewarded in His time. As you continue to faithfully serve, remember that you are part of something much greater than yourself a divine plan that spans eternity. Your dedication and faithfulness at the altar are seeds that will bear fruit, both in this life and in the life to come. Trust that God sees your labor, and His reward is sure.

Chapter 13

PRAYERS OF AN ALTAR WORKER

Who may ascend the mountain of the Lord? Who may stand in His holy place? The one who has clean hands and a pure heart, who does not trust in an idol or swear by a false god.
Psalm 24:3-4

Prayer is the foundation of every altar workers preparation. Before stepping into service, time spent in prayer is crucial to align the spirit with God's will. Prayer postures the heart in humility, reverence, and readiness to serve. It ensures that the altar worker is effective and guards against becoming a vessel that the enemy might use to hinder the flow of the Holy Spirit.

Prayer of Preparation

Heavenly Father, I come before Your throne through the access of the blood of Jesus. Thank You, Lord, for the privilege of serving at the altar.

I humble myself in Your presence I plead the blood of Jesus over my mind, heart, and spirit. I ask for complete cleansing and purification, that every part of me may be sanctified and set apart for Your work. Let the blood of Jesus cover me, protecting me from the plans of the enemy, and shield me from anything that would distract or hinder Your will.

Lord, I thank You for the honor of serving at Your altar. Create in me a clean heart, and renew a right spirit within me. Make me a vessel of honor, ready for the Master's use. Have Your way, Lord. Let Your will be done, and let Your kingdom come in this place where I have come to serve.

Holy Spirit, I yield to You. I submit to Your leading and guidance as I co-labor with You in the work of the Kingdom. Use me as a vessel of honor and glory for Your purposes. Let nothing in me hinder what You desire to accomplish today. Fill me with Your Spirit, that I may serve and be effective in for the kingdom.

Prayer for Protection and Authority

Father, in the name of Jesus, I take authority over every power of darkness that seeks to hinder Your work at this altar. I bind every spirit, every influence, and every work of the enemy that would attempt to disrupt the flow of the Holy Spirit. I reject every thought, attitude, or action that could quench Your work, diminish the sacredness of this moment, or dishonor Your presence.

I declare in the name of Jesus that no weapon formed against this altar or against me shall prosper. I plead the blood of Jesus, which speaks better things than the blood of Abel, releasing healing, deliverance, and restoration to all who come to You. Let Your power flow unhindered. In the mighty name of Jesus, Amen.

Prayer for the People

Heavenly Father, I lift up every individual who comes to this altar today. You know their hearts, their burdens, their desires, and their needs. I pray that You meet them at the point of their need. Let healing flow to the sick, deliverance to the oppressed, and comfort to the brokenhearted.

Let Your presence fill this place, saturating it with Your glory. May every person who encounters You here experience transformation, restoration, and empowerment. Let Your will be done in their lives, and may Your name be glorified in every heart that is touched.

Lord, I surrender this moment to You. Take full control, and have Your way. May every life be touched, renewed, and empowered according to Your perfect plan.

In Jesus mighty name, Amen.!

ABOUT THE AUTHOR

Nina Brown is an assistant Pastor and Author who has dedicated her life to serving the Lord. She serves at Christ Restoration Ministries International under the leadership of Bishop George Agbonson.

Nina's mission is to help others discover their God-given purpose and experience His transformative power.

Connect with Nina Brown:

Email: ninabrown22@yahoo.com

www.ingramcontent.com/pod-product-compliance
Lightning Source LLC
Chambersburg PA
CBHW060657280326
41933CB00012B/2224